aperture

The book is a circle
Made up of squares
Turn through the pages
Consider the pairs

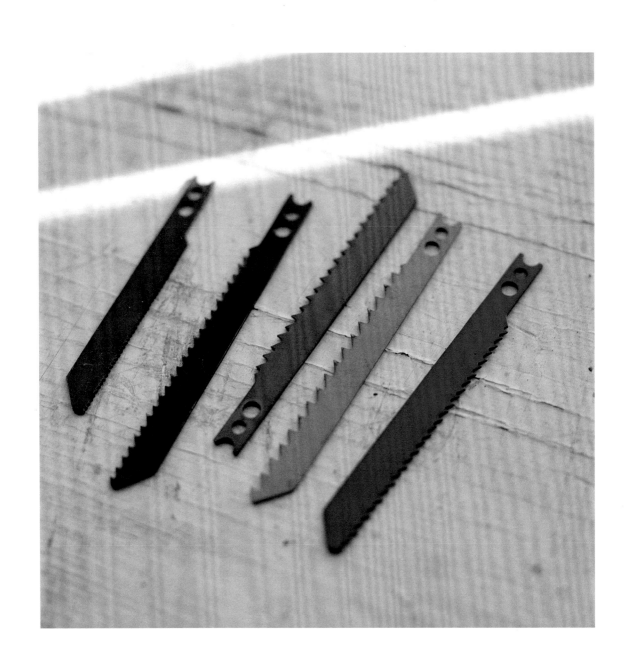

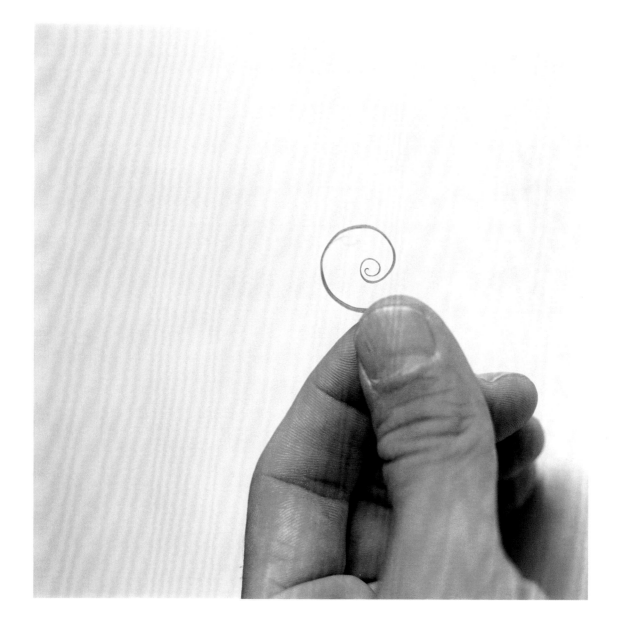

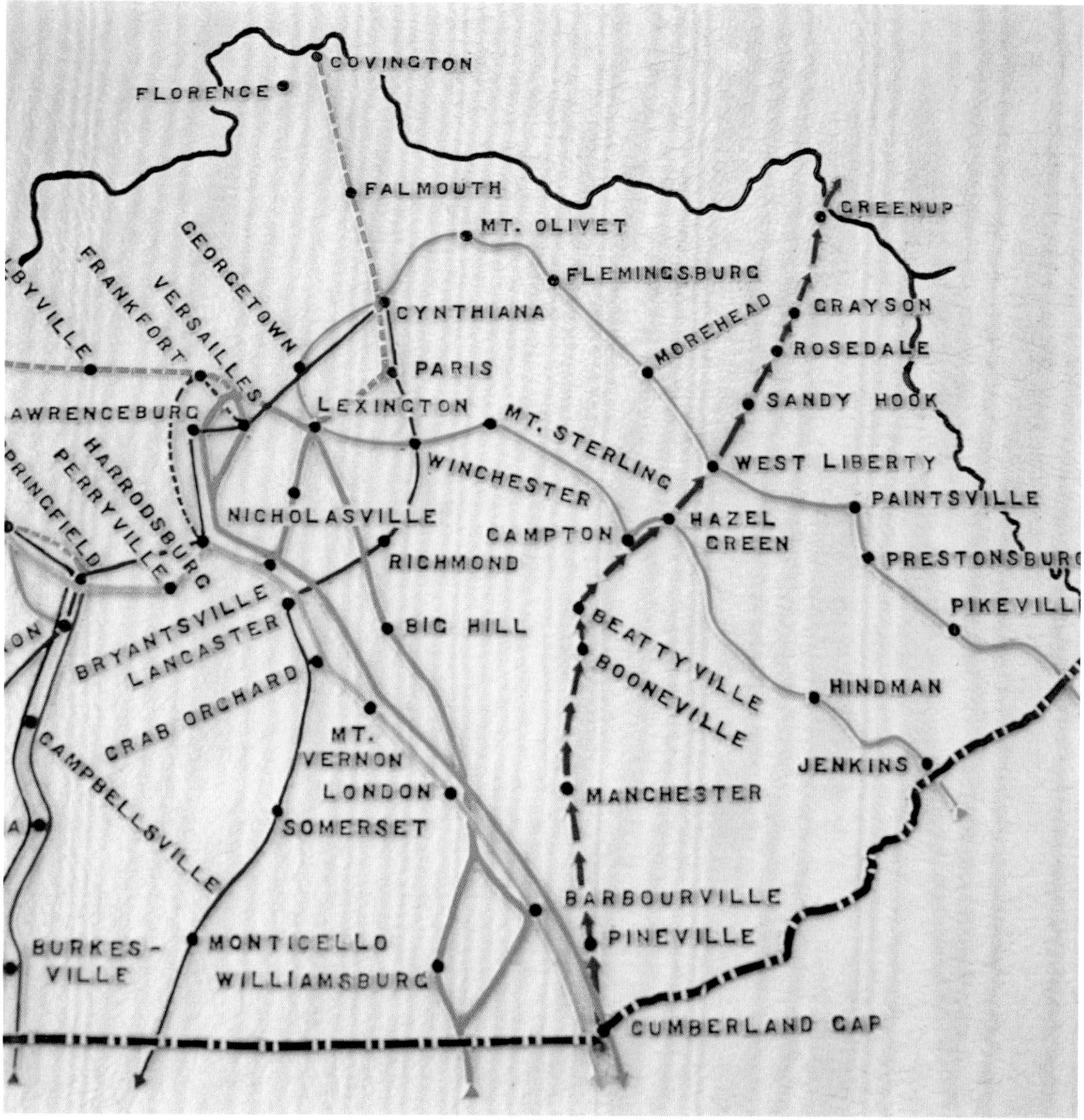

COVINGTON
FLORENCE
FALMOUTH
GREENUP
MT. OLIVET
FLEMINGSBURG
GEORGETOWN
FRANKFORT
VERSAILLES
CYNTHIANA
MOREHEAD
GRAYSON
ROSEDALE
PARIS
SANDY HOOK
LEXINGTON
MT. STERLING
HARRODSBURG
PERRYVILLE
WINCHESTER
WEST LIBERTY
PAINTSVILLE
NICHOLASVILLE
CAMPTON
HAZEL GREEN
RICHMOND
BRYANTSVILLE
LANCASTER
BEATTYVILLE
BIG HILL
BOONEVILLE
HINDMAN
CRAB ORCHARD
MT. VERNON
JENKINS
CAMPBELLSVILLE
LONDON
MANCHESTER
SOMERSET
BARBOURVILLE
BURKES-VILLE
MONTICELLO
PINEVILLE
WILLIAMSBURG
CUMBERLAND GAP

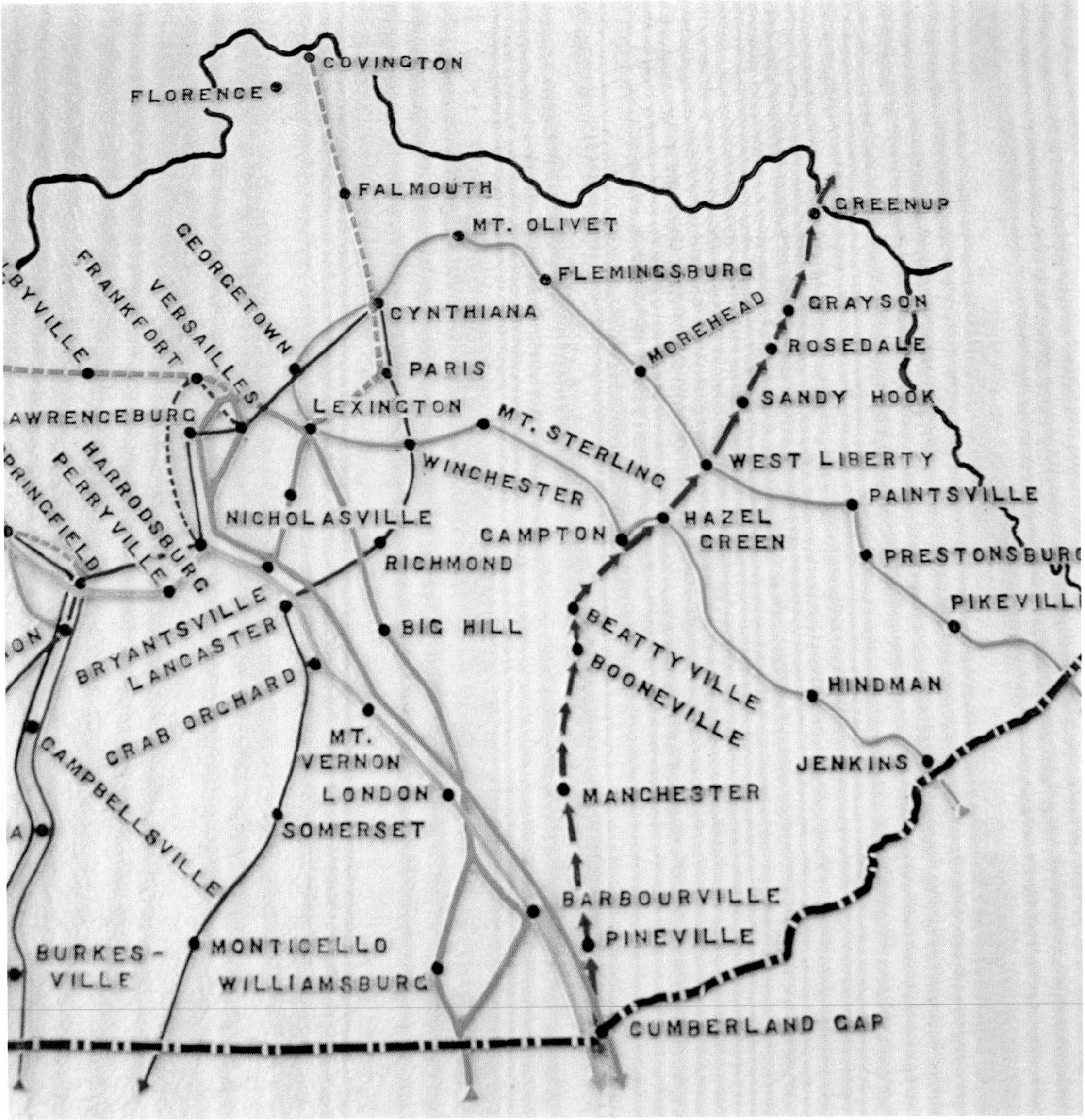

FLORENCE •   • COVINGTON

• FALMOUTH

MT. OLIVET

FLEMINGSBURG

GEORGETOWN

FRANKFORT

VERSAILLES

CYNTHIANA   GRAYSON

MOREHEAD

GREENUP

BYVILLE

PARIS   ROSEDALE

LEXINGTON   SANDY HOOK

LAWRENCEBURG   MT. STERLING   WEST LIBERTY

HARRODSBURG   WINCHESTER   PAINTSVILLE

SPRINGFIELD   PERRYVILLE   NICHOLASVILLE   HAZEL GREEN   PRESTONSBURG

CAMPTON   PIKEVILLE

RICHMOND

BRYANTSVILLE   BIG HILL   BEATTYVILLE

LANCASTER   BOONEVILLE   HINDMAN

ON   CRAB ORCHARD

MT.   JENKINS

CAMPBELLSVILLE   VERNON   MANCHESTER

LONDON

A   SOMERSET

BARBOURVILLE

BURKES-   MONTICELLO   PINEVILLE

VILLE   WILLIAMSBURG

CUMBERLAND GAP

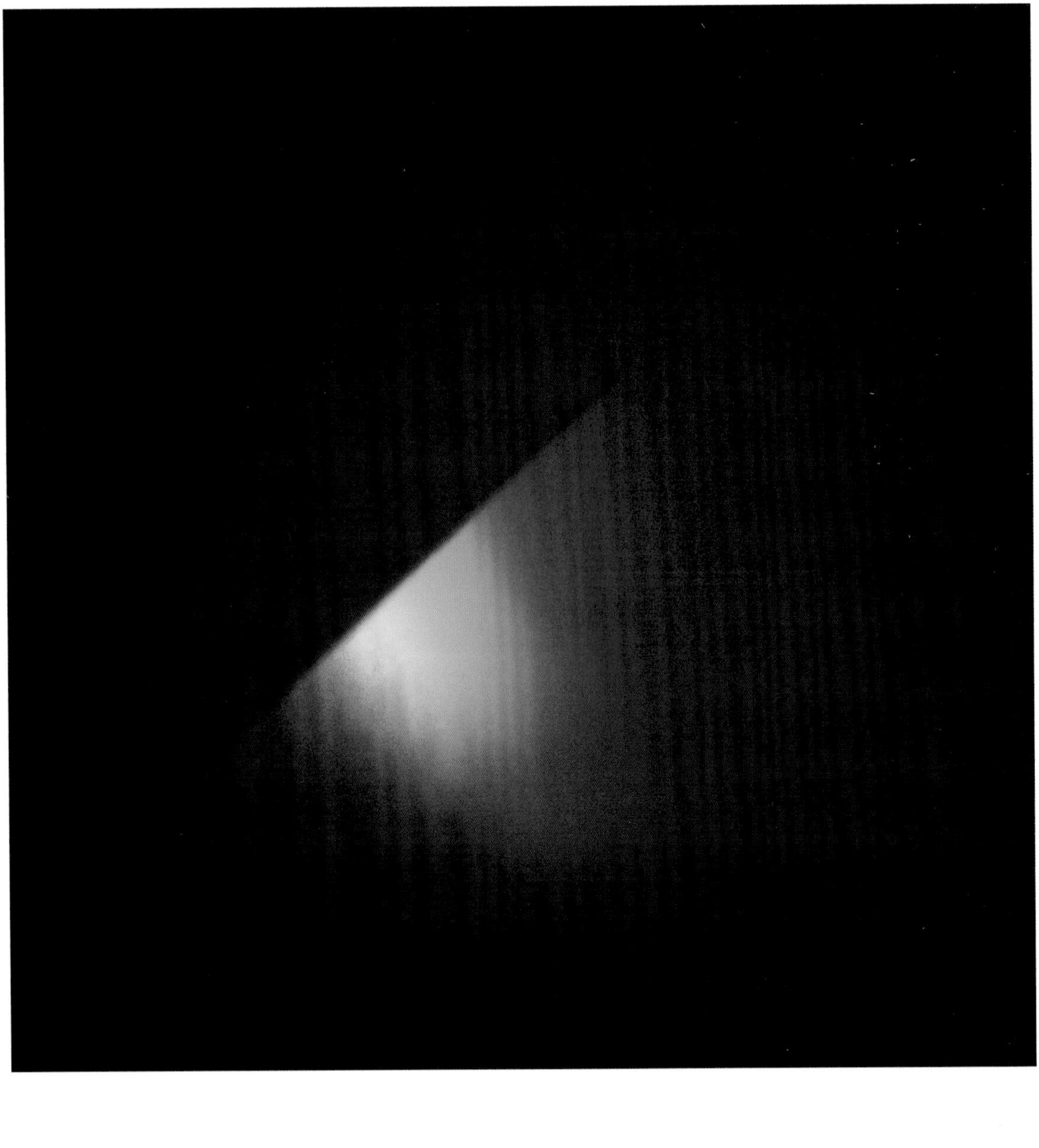

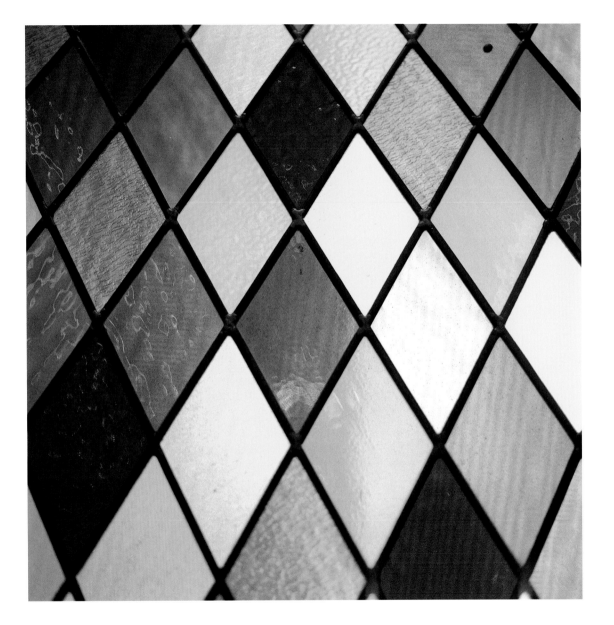

This Equals That
By Jason Fulford and Tamara Shopsin
Photographs by Jason Fulford

Editor: Denise Wolff
Editorial Assistant: Robyn Taylor
Designers: Jason Fulford and Tamara Shopsin
Production Manager: Matthew Harvey
Production Assistant: Luke Chase
Work Scholars: Natalie Ivis, Jessica Lancaster

Additional staff of the Aperture book program
includes: Chris Boot, Executive Director; Sarah
McNear, Deputy Director; Lesley A. Martin,
Publisher; Kellie McLaughlin, Director of Sales
and Marketing; Susan Ciccotti, Senior Text
Editor; Amelia Lang, Managing Editor; Madeline
Coleman, Copy Editor; Samantha Marlow,
Editorial Assistant

A learning guide for *This Equals That* is available
at aperture.org/educationalpublications

Children participating in Aperture's after-school
programs in underserved communities will each
receive a copy of *This Equals That*, made possible
by a grant from the Pinkerton Foundation and a
gift from Agnes Gund.

First edition
Printed in China
10 9 8 7 6 5 4 3 2 1

Library of Congress Control Number: 2014938759
ISBN 978-1-59711-288-8

Aperture Foundation books are distributed in the
U.S. and Canada by:
ARTBOOK/D.A.P.
155 Sixth Avenue, 2nd Floor
New York, N.Y. 10013
Phone: (212) 627-1999
Fax: (212) 627-9484
E-mail: orders@dapinc.com
www.artbook.com

Aperture Foundation books are distributed
worldwide, excluding the U.S. and Canada, by:
Thames & Hudson Ltd.
181A High Holborn
London WC1V 7QX
United Kingdom
Phone: + 44 20 7845 5000
Fax: + 44 20 7845 5055
E-mail: sales@thameshudson.co.uk
www.thamesandhudson.com

aperture

Aperture Foundation
547 West 27th Street, 4th Floor
New York, N.Y. 10001
www.aperture.org

Aperture, a not-for-profit foundation, connects
the photo community and its audiences with the
most inspiring work, the sharpest ideas, and with
each other—in print, in person, and online.